Battleships

Kate Riggs

CREATIVE EDUCATION • CREATIVE PAPERBACKS

Published by Creative Education and Creative Paperbacks
P.O. Box 227, Mankato, Minnesota 56002
Creative Education and Creative Paperbacks
are imprints of The Creative Company
www.thecreativecompany.us

Design by Ellen Huber; production by Chelsey Luther
Art direction by Rita Marshall
Printed in the United States of America

Photographs by Alamy (Greg Vaughn), Corbis (DAVID
MCNEW/Reuters), Dreamstime (Arinahabich08, Dave
Newman), Flickr (Antonio Turretto), Getty Images (Purestock,
Stocktrek Images, Peter Wilson), iStockphoto (beverett,
tropicalpixsingapore), Shutterstock (Vereshchagin Dmitry),
SuperStock (StockTrek/Purestock, Travel Pix Collection/Jon
Arnold Images), U.S. Navy (Daniel Barker, Michael D. Cole,
Jennifer Gold, Michael A. Lantron, Eli J. Medellin, Jacob D.
Moore)

Library of Congress Cataloging-in-Publication Data
Riggs, Kate.
Battleships / Kate Riggs.
p. cm. — (Seedlings)
Includes index.
Summary: A kindergarten-level introduction to battleships,
covering their captains, weapons, role in battle, and such
defining features as their decks.
ISBN 978-1-60818-660-0 (hardcover)
ISBN 978-1-62832-245-3 (pbk)
ISBN 978-1-56660-674-5 (eBook)
1. Battleships—Juvenile literature. I. Title.
V815.R54 2016
359.8'352—dc23   2015007561

CCSS: RI.K.1, 2, 3, 4, 5, 6, 7; RI.1.1,
2, 3, 4, 5, 6, 7; RF.K.1, 3; RF.1.1

First Edition HC 9 8 7 6 5 4 3 2 1
First Edition PBK 9 8 7 6 5 4 3 2 1

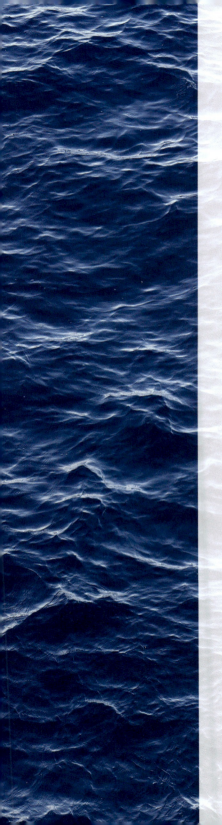

TABLE OF CONTENTS

Time to sail!

Powerful
warships
wage battle
at sea.

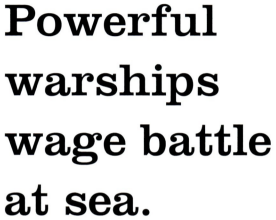

They keep other ships safe.

Long battleships are covered with **armor**.

Heavy guns are on the **deck**.

Part of the gun **turret** sticks above the deck. It can move around to fire.

People work
below the deck.
They load the
guns. They keep
the ship moving.

Many warships
follow battleships.

The battleship looks for danger. It speeds ahead.

A battleship cruises the seas. It aims at **targets**. It fires its powerful guns.

Go, battleship, go!

Picture a Battleship

antenna

gun barrels

forecastle

deck

hull

61

radar

bridge

stern

Words to Know

armor: a metal covering that keeps something safe

deck: the outside top level of a ship

targets: planes or ships that get shot at

turret: the tower on a battleship that holds a big gun

Read More

Bodden, Valerie. *Battleships*.
Mankato, Minn: Creative Education, 2012.

Bozzo, Linda. *U.S. Navy*.
Mankato, Minn.: Amicus, 2014.

Websites

Battleship Game
http://www.superkids.com/aweb/tools/logic/bship/
Play "Battleship" against the computer.

U.S. Navy Battleships
http://www.archives.gov/research/military/navy-ships
/battleships.html
Look at photos of early battleships.

Index

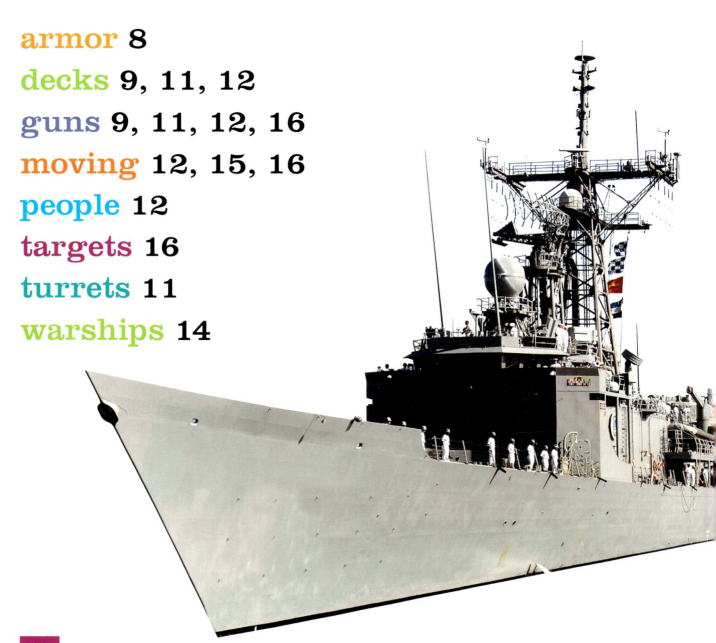